T0078032

My Night in Captivity

Spears Books
An Imprint of Spears Media Press LLC
7830 W. Alameda Ave, Suite 103-247
Denver, CO 80226
United States of America

First Published in the United States of America in 2021 by Spears Books
www.spearsmedia.com
info@spearsmedia.com
Information on this title: www.spearsmedia.com/my-night-in-captivity
© 2021 Christian Cardinal Wiyghan Tumi
All rights reserved.

ISBN: 9781942876731 (Paperback)
ISBN: 9781942876748 (eBook)
Also available in Kindle format

Cover designed by Doh Kambem
Designed and typeset by Spears Media Press LLC

Distributed worldwide by African Books Collective (ABC)
https://www.africanbookscollective.com

MY
NIGHT IN
CAPTIVITY

A Memoir

Christian Cardinal Wiyghan Tumi
With Martin Jumbam

Spears Books
Denver, Colorado

CONTENTS

List of Figures

FOREWORD

Social media had a field day of the Fon of Nso's home-coming, particularly the hectic welcome he received in Bamenda on November 5, 2020. Hundreds of Nso inhabitants of Bamenda town, together with their friends and obviously idle curiosity seekers, jammed the road along which the Fon was passing through, in the company of His Eminence Christian Cardinal Tumi, the Emeritus Archbishop of Douala. A long convoy of cars then escorted them to Bambili, some ten miles, or so, away, and then, to Cardinal Tumi's dismay, all turned round and drove back where they had come from. To him, that was an act of "abandonment", which immediately brought an ominous feeling of something bad about to happen to them, and happened, it did! They descended the Sabga hill onto the Ndop plain right into the waiting arms of the so-called "Amba boys" of Ndop.

News of their capture took social media by storm; understandably so, given the importance of the personalities involved, that is, a traditional ruler of no mean stature, and a Cardinal of the Roman Catholic Church.

What a dramatic catch for the "Amba boys"! What a valuable bargaining chip they believed they had in their hands, and they tried to make the best of their newfound notoriety, as Cardinal Tumi so clearly illustrates in this slim publication.

Therein, the reader learns of the intense behind-the-scenes negotiations that had dragged over several months, as Nso notables and other elders tried to convince a rather reluctant Fon of Nso that it was high time he ended his years in internal exile and return home to his people. The question of why, despite such a media-intensive publicity, the Fon's homecoming was still not shadowed by a military escort is answered when we learn that the regional governor did indeed make such an offer, which was politely turned down, and why.

The Cardinal tells of how much he relished the opportunity offered him during his one-night ordeal in the hands of his captors, not only to educate them on the necessity of allowing our children to go back to school, but also to send a clear message to the powers-that-be, which have always suspected him of complicity with the "Amba boys", that now is the time to silence the guns and bring back the peace our people so long for.

Martin Jumbam

CHAPTER 1

How it all Began

The news that I had been kidnapped went viral in a matter of minutes, thanks to my captors, who quickly beamed it to the entire world through social media. As soon as they realised who I was, they knew they had a powerful bargaining chip in their hands. They were excited, they told me, that I would serve as their mouthpiece to deliver their message, not only to what they called "La République", but to the entire world. In a space of a few months, I had gone from a peace crusader to a captive in the hands of a group that could easily have executed me, if they had so desired. How did that happen? A historical perspective is certainly in order here.

My ardent quest for peace to return to the North West and South West Regions of Cameroon dates to the onset of what has now become known as the "Anglophone Crisis". As the said crisis picked up steam, with neither side (the government or the so-called "Amba boys") seemingly willing to listen to each other, I invited a group of religious leaders from the two affected regions to meet in Douala for us to see what we could do as moral authorities to silence the sounds of the guns, already gaining in intensity in our land. The initial team around me included the Right Reverend Fonki Samuel Forba, the Moderator of the Presbyterian Church in Cameroon, El Hadj Tukur Mohammed Adamu, the Imam of the Bamenda Central Mosque, and El Hadj Mohammed Aboubaca, the Imam of the Buea Central Mosque. I also invited a world-renowned scholar, Dr Simon Munzu, who served as the coordinator of our meetings.

FIGURE 1.1. Some members of the Anglophone General Conference

Prior to the creation of this group, I had taken time to listen to the views of a number of Anglophones at home and abroad on this crisis and found them alarmingly divergent. That is why I thought that some of us, religious leaders, preferably those already retired from active duty, could come together and reflect on the causes of the crisis at hand and propose possible solutions to them. I told them that, given our positions as moral and religious authorities, we could not remain indifferent to the plight of our people, who were beginning to suffer enormous hardships from the war that was gaining ground in our part of the country.

FIGURE 1.2. Dr Simon Munzu, Anglophone General Conference Coordinator

That was how the Anglophone General Conference saw the light of day. I have heard some people referring to it as the "All Anglophone Conference (AAC)-III."

The first "All Anglophone Conference (AAC)-I" met at the Mount Mary premises in Buea "from 2nd to 3rd April 1993, for the purpose of preparing Anglophone participation in the forthcoming National Debate on Constitutional reform and of examining a variety of other issues relating to the welfare of ourselves, our posterity, our territory and our country as a whole (…)". Among the most pressing demands was "the return of Cameroon to the Federal form of Government."[1]

Nothing came out of it and from April 29 through May 2, 1994, another "All Anglophone Conference was held in the North West Provincial capital of Bamenda to consider, among other things, the implications for Anglophone Cameroon of the BIYA Government's arbitrary suspension for nearly one year of the constitutional reform process initiated in November 1992."[2]

In our case, I was eager to see the formation of an Anglophone political party that could fight for our cause within the constituted boundaries laid down by the laws of our land. Prior to the envisaged conference, we deemed it wise to consult Anglophones at home and in the diaspora through a questionnaire that contained three questions only:

1. What are the root causes of our problems?
2. What solutions do you envisage for them?
3. Having observed the behaviour of the army and the so-called "Amba boys" on the ground, should moral education be introduced in our schools?

1. The Buea Declaration issued by the All Anglophone Conference held in Buea on 2nd and 3rd April 1993, p. 1.
2. The Bamenda Proclamation issued by the All Anglophone Conference meeting in its second session in Bamenda from 29th April to 1st May 1994, p.1.

I made it clear that moral education should, in no way, be construed as meaning Catholic education, but should be seen rather as the religion of the children's parents; in other words, the Bible for Christians, the Koran for Muslims, and those without any religious inclinations would choose what side to lean on. Of all those questions, the one that received an overwhelming response from the public was the one on the importance of moral education in our educational system: 92% of the respondents were in favour of it.

With the responses from our questionnaire, we produced an over 400-page document, which we sent directly to President Paul Biya, urging him, among other things, to convene a common assembly in which the Anglophone problems could be debated. We booked an appointment for me to meet him to discuss the matter in detail, but we never received any response to our request.

We then decided to meet among ourselves as Anglophones in the historic city of Buea. Unfortunately, a number of obstacles stood on our path. First of all, we applied for an authorisation from the government to hold our meeting, which was never granted. Secondly, the then Mayor of Buea, Mr. Patrick Ekema, vowed that, even if the government were to grant us permission to meet, he would not allow us to meet in Buea. He asked us to take our meeting to Bamenda. Since we did not want any confrontation with him, we took his advice and contacted the Senior Divisional Officer for Mezam to authorise us to meet in Bamenda, but he, in turn, politely advised us to hold our meeting in Douala instead.

We were still hunting for a venue for our meeting when President Paul Biya took the wind out of our sails by convening the "Major National Dialogue" to which some of us were invited. Since our intention in the first place had been to see peace return to our part of the country at all costs, some of us accepted his invitation and I even chaired one of the commissions on the reconstruction of those areas of our regions that have been destroyed, so our people could return home.

CHAPTER 2

Crisis in Nsoland

The Major National Dialogue has come and gone, yet the situation on the ground in many parts of Anglophone Cameroon has not improved. Innocent men, women and children are still dying in the hands of both the military and the armed opposition factions. One such place that has been badly affected by the present crisis is Bui Division of the North West Region, where I come from. The extent of the destruction in lives and property is indescribable. The Diocese of Kumbo has extensively documented the extent of the deaths and destruction of property in its area of jurisdiction.

One person, who has borne the full force of the crisis is the Paramount Fon of Nso, Sehm Mbinglo I. He was kidnapped on two occasions and held captive before being released. Two of his sons were killed under circumstances that have never been clearly elucidated. Some of the Fon's detractors accuse him of being too involved with the government. Some even claim that he has been urging his people to support the ruling party. He fell ill and was flown out of Nso to Yaounde where a son of Nso, General Ivo Yenwo, graciously received him in his home.

Where I came into Picture

A few months ago, General Yenwo, who is from Nso, like me, called to inform me of the initiative by Nso notables (*vibai* and *shufais*) to convince the Fon of Nso to go back home. The Fon's presence in the General's house was becoming an embarrassment, not only to the General himself but also to the Nso traditional rulers. According to Nso tradition, the Fon should never be absent from the palace for so long. The General had generously agreed to host him for what he thought was going to be a short stay. Unfortunately, the conditions at home continued to degenerate and what was meant to be a short stay ended up being an embarrassingly long one.

From our discussion, I felt the awkward position the General and the Nso notables were in because of the Fon's presence in his house. I was told that the General is not the right person traditionally under whose roof the Fon of Nso should take shelter. Only a member of the *Nwerong* house, the traditional guardian of the royal family, should host the Fon. My understanding is that General Yenwo is not of that lineage. He had, out of the goodness of his heart, agreed to receive the Fon only because of the emergency circumstances under which the Fon had left his palace.

FIGURE 2.1. His Royal Highness, Fon Sehm Mbinglo I, Paramount Fon of Nso

CHAPTER 3

Absentee Fon!

With the situation at home gradually improving, it was therefore understandable that the gracious host was beginning to find the Fon a cumbersome guest. He wondered what he would tell the Nso people if, for example, something bad were to happen to their Fon under his roof? He therefore contacted the Nso traditional authorities (*nwerong*, *shufais* and *vibai*), who agreed with him that the Fon had to go back home.

For his part, however, the Fon still nurtured the fear that some people were out to kill him and so was not too eager to go back home. That was when it was decided that contacts be made with the other elders of Nso society, civil and religious, living outside Nso, to seek their help to convince the Fon to go back home. Such an effort had to be an all-Nso endeavour, with no assistance sought from outside the Nso community.

I was, therefore, one of the persons General Yenwo contacted for my views on the initiative that was already underway for the Fon to go back to his palace. I had no objection to his approach since I am one of the oldest Nso people alive today, having just celebrated my 90th birthday anniversary. Being on retirement, and with no pastoral commitments to hold me down, I accepted to attend the meeting convened at the General's residence with the other elders of the land and the Fon himself. The first meeting took place in September 2020.

Inquiring further, I learnt that the idea that the Fon should return to his palace was not something that just came up at the spur of the moment. For long, Nso people of all walks of life had been eager to have him back home but somehow no one really had the courage to bring it up in the open, or even to discuss it with other people. At what stage the traditional elders decided that the issue be discussed in the open, I do not know. But by the time I came into the picture, discussions around the Fon's return home were already in the open.

One reason I felt the notables of the land wanted me in the discussions was the success I had earlier in convincing the *Shufai* Tsenla in Kikaikelaki, the head of my paternal household, to go back to his people. He had been living in Douala from the time these unfortunate events began in Nsoland.

I happened to have been in Kikai sometime early in the year and after Holy Mass, a good number of *shufais* and *fais* and other elders of the locality came to greet me. I asked them how they were faring, and they all unanimously told me that they were now without a head.

Shufai Tsenla, whom they all consider their leader, had fled the events at home and they felt that his absence constituted a hindrance to the return of peace to the village. During the few days I spent at the Kikai parish, I heard the same message from just about everyone I talked to.

When I came back to Douala, *Shufai* Tsenla himself came to see me. Prior to being made the head of the Tsenla family, he was living in Douala and working as a tailor. So, when the disturbances at home intensified, he came back to Douala where his wife was still residing. When he asked me how things were at home, I repeated just what his people had told me, that Kikai village no longer had anyone at its head. He was profoundly touched by what he heard. In fact, he sat in silence for a long time and then asked me what I thought he should do. I told him, "Go back to your people. You are a leader, and a leader should never abandon his people, especially in moments of such grave difficulties. Be with them in their suffering and in their joy. They need you."

Even though he went back rather reluctantly, he was startled by the overwhelming welcome he received on arrival. He later told me that when word went out that he was returning home, the population of Kumbo as a whole, not only those from Kikai, came out in full force to welcome him. He later told me that people lined up from the Bui river all the way to Tsenla, several miles away. When he arrived in his compound, it was already packed full with a joyous crowd that applauded his arrival.

He also recounted an incident that occurred when some "Amba boys" appeared, firing their guns in the air. People, believing that the soldiers and the "Amba boys" were engaging in a battle, fled in disarray, only coming back when they realised that the "Amba boys" too had come out to share in the joy of welcoming their *Shufai* home. Those were the very boys he had fled the village in fear of; there they were, joining the people to welcome him back home. From that moment, he became convinced that the people were yearning for the return of all traditional rulers, who had abandoned their people at the height of this war, notably the Fon of Nso. Since *Shufai* Tsenla is one of the Fon's top advisers, he was at the forefront of negotiations to convince the Fon, reluctant though he was, to go back home.

CHAPTER 4

Negotiating the Fon's Return Home

We had the first meeting in Yaounde in September 2020. I had been in Kumbo, where the Bishop had decided to celebrate my 90th birthday ahead of time. It was there that I received the invitation to join the elders who were going to Yaounde to bring back their Fon.

So, I left Kumbo directly for Yaounde where I met the Nso notables and General Yenwo all assembled around their Fon. I was touched by their eagerness and strong determination to have their Fon back in his palace. As I listened to all that was being said, and how it was said, I became aware of how little I knew of Nso society. I was also stunned that I did not know as much Lamnso as I have always thought I did. They spoke in proverbs, idioms, and understatements that they all seemed to understand so well but which I had difficulty understanding. As the discussions were going on, I was surprised by the Fon's silence. You could have thought all that discussion did not concern him at all. He sat at one corner in total silence, saying very little, but seemingly listening intently to all that was being said.

As I watched and listened, I wondered if he was really ready to go back home. I was therefore not surprised when some elders whispered to me that he was under the influence of one of his young wives, who was said to be resolutely against him going back to Nso. She reportedly claimed that the Fon was being lured back home to be assassinated, a thought the elders found understandably irritating. There was, however, some speculation among the elders that she, and some people around the Fon, who did not want him to go back, had their own ulterior motives. It was rumoured that the Fon's presence in Yaounde was already attracting many visitors and sympathisers, who never came to visit the Fon empty-handed. It would therefore seem that economic motives were behind her stance. I never personally talked with her to know why she thought the Fon was being lured back home to his death. From every indication, she is said to be of a younger generation and is reportedly well-educated as well. Understandably, some of the elders were quite upset by what they saw as the insidious female influence behind the throne that was responsible for the Fon's reluctance to go home.

When it seemed that not much progress was being made, the Fon maintaining a stony silence, I asked some of them what would happen if the Fon categorically refused to go back. They told me that they had two options: one was to take him back home by force

– although they never said how that could be done practically; the other option – one that seemed more feasible – would be for *nwerong* to dethrone him by declaring the throne vacant and installing someone else in his place.

As I listened to the Nso notables speak, one thing that struck me forcefully, was how very well organised the Nso society is. I would agree with those who say that it is one of the oldest and best well organised societies in the grassfield region of Cameroon. Nothing seems to be left to chance. I could feel the intense desire of the Nso people to have their Fon back, as expressed through their leaders. They made it expressly clear that the highest office of the land could not remain vacant because its occupant had chosen a life in exile.

CHAPTER 5

The Fon Agrees to Go Back Home

As the discussions were gaining in intensity, the Fon seemed to realise that he had no choice but to go back home. For the first time, he spoke and said he had heard his people's wishes and that he would be going back home. What a relief we all felt! The notables all rose from their seats, clapped their hands as tradition demands, cupped them and brought them to their mouths as they shouted praises to their Fon. They called him *nchang-nchang*, *nginyam*, *bvereh* (lion), *shui-nso* (the sun shining on the Nso people), *nyui-Nso* (the god of the Nso people). I was wondering why anyone would refer to the Fon as *nyui-Nso*, a title I found quite strange, but the Sultan of Foumban would later explain to me that prior to the arrival of the missionaries, the Fon was an all-powerful figure; no one, or nothing, was thought to be above him, hence the people equated him with one of their gods.

The excitement caused by the Fon's acceptance to return home was soon dampened when he suddenly had a change of mind. He said that since the palace had been abandoned for a long time, it was no longer in a condition that he could live in. He said he would only go back home on condition that the palace was properly cleaned. Although the notables were all saddened when they realised the Fon's determination not to go back home with them on that day, they nonetheless agreed that they would return to Kumbo and ensure that the renovation work in the palace was carried out. We then agreed to meet again at a date to be determined.

Two months later, in November 2020, we were again back in Yaounde. It was quite convenient for me because I happened to be in Yaounde for another occasion, so I took the opportunity to be present at the second meeting. It was now just a question of how the Fon's return was going to happen in practical terms.

After further discussion, it was agreed that we would travel the next day in a convoy. The Fon opted to ride in my car accompanied by his wife and his valet (*nchelav*). I did not object to that arrangement. We all separated for the night, happy that a solution had at last been found and that the Fon would be home the next day. Early in the morning, we all left in a convoy, with the Fon on the back seat of my car and those accompanying him on the middle seat, while I sat ahead with my driver. At last, we were heading directly for Kumbo, or so I thought.

CHAPTER 6

The Fon Refuses to Go Beyond Foumban

We drove in almost total silence from Yaounde to Bafoussam. Occasionally, the Fon would briefly say something to his valet (*nchelav*), or to his wife, and then silence. It was only several hours into the journey that the Fon said something to me that I did not understand. His wife then told me that he was offering me a piece of cake, which I politely accepted.

On the whole, I usually do not talk much when I am travelling, even with my driver, and so the silence in the car was nothing strange to me. It was also understandable because the Fon of Nso and I had never had much to say to each other, given that he is not someone I am particularly close to. In the past, each time I went home, I always paid him a visit; that was before he became a Muslim. After his conversion to Islam, I decided to respect his decision by steering clear of the palace and so our contacts had been minimal, at best. It was only recently, with the negotiations to have him back to the palace, that we again exchanged a few words, which were mainly words of greetings. Even if I had wanted to talk to him, I would not have known what to say. It was clear that he too was only too happy to avoid saying anything to me. That was made easier as my car is long and he was sitting way at the back and directly behind me, which made any conversation, even if we felt like having any, difficult.

When we arrived in Bafoussam, the Fon suddenly said that he could not drive past without paying a courtesy visit to the Sultan of Foumban, El Hadj Mbombo Njoya. That was not on our original plan as the initial agreement had been to head directly for Kumbo. The notables themselves were understandably alarmed but, after a brief discussion, they agreed that we stop at the Sultan's palace for a brief visit.

The Sultan very graciously received us and I was assigned a room in a house a distance away from the main palace building for some rest. The Sultan came over to greet me and we talked briefly before he left. He said he was preparing a trip to Yaounde for some party issues. He then bade me goodbye and left. He was barely away for a few minutes when he rushed back, looking visibly worried. I asked what the matter was and he said there was a problem: his wife had just informed him that the Fon of Nso's wife had just told her that our intention was to take the Fon home to be killed. As such, the Fon had decided that he would not be going up to Kumbo with us.

Not only was I stunned by what I heard, I was frankly

furious. I immediately went to the Fon to tell him to consider the gravity of what he was saying. Did he really believe that I, Cardinal Tumi, and all the elders of the land were taking him back to be killed? I told the Sultan how sad I was to see that the Fon could believe what his wife was saying. I could not believe that he, the Fon, could associate me, and the elders of our people, in a plot to eliminate him. From every indication, his wife seemed to wield considerable influence over him. She managed to convince him that our intention was to have him killed. I felt sad and sorry for him at the same time. That was an issue I thought we had resolved once and for all back in Yaounde. Why it resurfaced again in Foumban was baffling to me.

Once the other members of the convoy learnt of the Fon's intention not to go beyond Foumban, they were at first speechless as they looked at each other totally puzzled, then they all became visibly furious with the Fon. It took us several hours of negotiations, with the firm intervention of the Sultan, before he agreed to continue his trip home. The Sultan told him that if he had not been on his way to Yaounde, he would have personally accompanied him up to his palace. The fact that the Sultan was willing to accompany him to Nso himself showed me that he (the Sultan) did not believe the conspiracy theory that was being peddled by the Fon's wife.

Finally, the Fon agreed to continue his journey home on condition that he spent the night in Foumban and only travel the next day. Reluctantly, the notables agreed that we could all spend the night and leave for Kumbo early the next morning. Just as everyone was heaving a sigh of relief that the brief crisis had been resolved, the Fon again raised another issue. Since the next day in the Nso calendar was a *ngoilum*, he said Nso tradition forbids the Fon from leaving the palace on that day. The elders again went into an emergency meeting to examine the Fon's new objection to travelling home. They came back to tell him that he was misinterpreting that law, which, it is true, requires that the Fon not leave the palace on *ngoilum*. However, the said law does not forbid the Fon, if he happens to be out of Nso, from coming back on a *ngoilum*. They made it clear that entering Nso and leaving the palace once in Nso were two different issues altogether. As such, his going home would not be in violation of the traditional edict that keeps any Fon grounded in the palace on a *ngoilum*.

As all those negotiations were going on, I merely watched and admired the diplomatic way with which our people resolve complicated matters that can bring conflict among people. No sooner had that issue been resolved than the Fon gave another condition, this time more manageable: he asked that the others go ahead of us and inform the population that he would be arriving the next day, *ngoilum*. The notables were not at all happy that the Fon was still dragging his feet by coming up with one excuse after another not to go up with them. It was then that I stepped in to calm tempers down, and offered to personally accompany the Fon the next day up to Kumbo. With that reassurance, they agreed, very reluctantly though, to go ahead of us through Jakiri to Kumbo. When they arrived in Kumbo, the *nwerong* announced in the market square that their Fon was on his way home. From that moment, I felt the weight of the people's expectations of their Fon's arrival entirely on my shoulders. It was not an easy mission but one that had to be accomplished, come rain, come shine.

FIGURE 6.1. El Hadj Ibrahim Mbombo Njoya, Sultan of the Bamum people

CHAPTER 7

Bamenda Welcomes the Fon

The next morning, we left Foumban for Kumbo through Bamenda. We drove in total silence through Bafoussam to Bamenda. When we arrived at the Bamenda Station, we went to pay our respects to the Governor. As we were getting into town, I called him to let him know we would like to meet him as we were on our way to Kumbo. He asked that we meet him at his residence because he does not go to his office on Mondays. When we met him, I had the feeling that he was not too happy that we were going up to Kumbo on that day. He did not say so openly but he kept talking about how rough "those boys were" and I could feel that he was not sure our going up to Nso was such a good idea. He, however, did not intervene and we left.

The Fon asked that we pass through Cow Street in downtown Bamenda. What I saw there took me completely by surprise. Hundreds of Nso people lined the street to greet us. It was a delight to see the number of dances present and, for the first time since we left Yaounde, I felt the genuine warmth of a people, who were truly yearning to have their ruler back on his throne. We, however, agreed that the Fon would not leave the car but that he would greet the people by waving at them through the car window. No sooner had we arrived among the people, than the Fon asked that we spend the night in Bamenda. I told him that it would not be a good idea at all, as his people were already anxiously waiting for him at home. His wife and *nchelav* agreed with me, and so he gave in and spoke briefly to the crowd from the car, and we left.

As we were about to leave town, the Divisional Officer of Kumbo arrived with a message from the Governor, offering us a military escort, if we so desired. I conveyed the Governor's message to the Fon and waited for him to say the final word. He turned down the offer and his wife and *nchelav* concurred with his decision. So I told the Governor's envoy to thank the Governor but that we would not accept his offer. By declining the offer of protection from the government, the Fon was complying with the decision made earlier in Yaounde during the negotiations for his homecoming. We had all agreed that it should not be construed as a government-led initiative. It had to remain an entirely Nso affair. Even the Bishop of Kumbo, Monsignor George Nkuo, also felt that we should leave the government out of it.

When the Governor made his offer, I wanted the Fon to be the one to make the final decision. Had he accepted the offer, that would have been fine by me. But when he, of his own freewill, turned it down, I welcomed his decision made in all sovereignty. The fact that he, his wife and valet jointly rejected the idea of a military escort, made me wonder if any of them, his wife included, really believed in the conspiracy theory she was spreading about us planning to eliminate her husband. If they sincerely believed what she was saying, that would have been, it seemed to me, an ideal opportunity to seek military protection.

CHAPTER 8

Into "Amba" Hands

A large delegation of Nso people accompanied us to the Bambili junction, some ten miles, or so, outside Bamenda, and then turned back. I was surprised they decided to leave us there, because I had been made to believe that a delegation from Bamenda would accompany the Fon all the way to his palace in Kumbo, sixty miles north of Bamenda.

As soon as the Bamenda delegation turned their back on us, I felt a certain loneliness. There I was alone with the Fon, and a few other people, who all looked up to me to get them home safely. And, frankly, I did not know how I was going to do that. I then began to wonder if we had been right not to accept the Governor's offer. A strange feeling of abandonment suddenly descended on me and I had the premonition that something bad was going to happen to us. It was already around 4PM and it was clear that we would be arriving in Kumbo at night. But there was no turning back; we had to go.

We went up the Bambili hill and down Sabga hill onto the Ndop plain on the other side. We drove all the way past Ndop town, past the school run by Reverend Sisters and there, around a corner, a number of young men, armed to the teeth, stopped us and ordered us out of the car. I told them that it was not possible for me to come down as quickly as they wanted me to. David, my driver, fearing that the fellows might try to force me out of the car, quickly left his seat and rushed to my side. He almost entered into a struggle with one of them whom he believed was touching me. The fellow pointed his gun at him and I quickly intervened and asked him not to resist. As soon as I had been helped out of the car, two other fellows joined my driver to place me on a bike. David was ordered to sit behind me, and we were taken through a bushy path to an abandoned house some miles away from the road.

The Fon and the other passengers were also brought on bikes to the same house. Shortly thereafter, the Fon, his wife and his *nchelav* were taken away and David and I were left alone. It was already late at night when we were again taken on a bike for another destination. Since it was already pitch dark, we could not say for sure where we were. We must have gone several kilometres into the bush through very rough and tiny paths. At one point, our biker suddenly stopped and announced that his "commanding officer" had asked him to drop us there in the bush. I asked if he was serious about leaving us in the bush and he said 'yes', that he had been asked to drop us there, but to remain with us pending further instructions. Just then, another biker arrived and led the way to another abandoned farmhouse. There was no light and we had to use our phone torches to see anything. There were some old chairs on which we sat. They asked if they could bring us some rice to eat and I refused. It was already too late at night to think of eating, and I was not sure what type of food they would serve us under such conditions.

I told them I could not sit up on a chair all night long, no matter how comfortable such a chair was. They then went out and came back with a light, old and torn mattress which they placed on the bare floor, and it was on it that I spent the night. I might as well have been sleeping on the bare floor itself, so thin the mattress was that I was practically lying on the cold, dusty floor. I only had my soutane on and nothing else to cover. To say that it was an uncomfortable night would be understating the matter. It was pure torture. But I was so tired that I must have slept for a few hours.

My Gratitude to my Driver

When I woke up after a few hours of sleep, I saw my driver, David, practically sitting up all night long. I was profoundly touched by his attachment to my person and I take this opportunity to thank him immensely for it. He was willing to sacrifice his life to ensure that nothing happened to me. The slightest act towards me that seemed to him to be out of place, or anything said to me, or about me, which he did not appreciate, he immediately reacted. When I was being pulled out of the car, for example, he jumped from his seat and rushed towards the fellow who was laying his hands on me, and I had to intervene forcefully for him to back down, as those fellows were already pointing their guns at him, and I was afraid he could be killed. I told him to think more of his wife and child than of me, an already old man, but he refused and stood by me throughout the ordeal. They wanted to separate us but he refused to leave me and the boys had to give in, and I was surprised they gave in so easily. He told them he knew my material needs, the medicines I take, and that he would not leave me. Finally, our captors caved in and he and I spent the night in the same abandoned house. May God bless him!

FIGURE 8.1. My driver, David Ngong Nsotaka (Tah Nyang)

As I sat in darkness, I began to reflect on what had just happened to us. It all looked surreal. Was I dreaming, or had we just been kidnapped? However, it did not take long for the hordes of mosquitoes to remind me that we were indeed captives of a group that said it was fighting to "free us from foreign domination." Some of them kept guard outside the door throughout the night. In moments like those, you wonder if dawn would ever come at all. But come, it did, and we saw more of our captors coming around and peeping into the house to look at us.

CHAPTER 9

The Interrogation that Went Viral

One of our captors, whom I assume was their commander, came and began questioning me, a scene they carefully videotaped and posted online for the whole world to watch. I told them that I would not answer any questions if they did not tell me what they had done with the Fon of Nso and the people with him. They looked at each other and I saw that they were hesitating to talk. I again made it clear that if they wanted me to talk, they would first tell me where he was. That is when they said the Fon of Nso was of no interest to them. As far as they were concerned, he was of interest only to the Nso people.

"We have handed him over to the 'Nso Warriors' and it is left to them to do with their Fon what they like. They are judging him for the crimes he committed in Nsoland, and what they decide to do to him, or with him, is of no concern to us here in Baba." They, however, assured me that by the time we reached Kumbo, the Fon would already be in his palace, which proved false.

When I heard that the Fon was already being taken to Kumbo, I then agreed to listen to them. They began by accusing me of illegally entering their territory without obtaining proper clearance from their high command. I said it was strange to hear them talking of proper clearance through a road I have used for years which, as far as I am concerned, is a public road. They told me I was mistaken because I was now in a new territory controlled by the "Amba boys".

"We know you as a great figure in this Southern Cameroons," they continued, "but we also know that you are a troublemaker. You have been urging the "Ambazonia Restoration Forces" to lay down their arms, and those who have agreed to lay down their arms have been killed by the "La Republique" forces."

"I have been accused of many things in this country, even by the government, but this is the first time I am being accused of luring your people to surrender their arms only to be killed. I, however, want to make it abundantly clear that my wish has always been to see, not only you lay down your arms but for the army also to go back to the barracks for peace to return to our land." They looked at each other and seemed confused by my honest talk and tone of voice.

"We have also heard," their leader continued, "that you are for a federation."

"Oh, yes, that is true," I said, before adding, "I am a Cameroonian citizen and a pastor to boot, and I have the pastoral obligation to speak the truth and to speak it freely, anywhere, anytime, to whoever is listening to me. I will tell anyone who is wrong that he or she is wrong, whether the individual in question represents the government or a member of your own groups fighting against the government. I am for a federation, not separation. I firmly believe that our country should remain one but split up into federated states. The number of such states is not for me to determine. I will say this to anyone, anywhere and at anytime. That is my stand and I assume whatever consequences may come from it." There was silence. Then their leader said: "We are particularly interested in you because you are an international figure and we know that what you say, the world will hear about it, listen and take action. We want you to tell "La Republique" and the whole world that we are not terrorists as the government is saying. We are freedom fighters, fighting for our land."

I told them that I am my own person and that I would not agree to be used as someone else's mouthpiece. Early that morning, I had heard some of them whispering outside the house they kept me in, saying that the whole world was already talking about me and, as such, they should be careful how they treated me.

My interrogators continued to say that they had nothing against me personally; that they had not captured me but had merely taken me into custody because I had entered their territory without proper clearance. They asked if I had anything to say about their struggle for independence.

I told them I did not agree with them on three points.

"First of all, your intolerance. You think that you are right in all that you do, and that you alone know what is good for our country. That is why anyone who disagrees with you has to die. How can you build a country," I asked, "by killing people simply because they disagree with your own vision of how the society should be governed?" I made it clear to them that their intolerance and brutality against those who disagree with them were unacceptable in any civilised society.

"No one has the monopoly of the truth," I continued, before adding, "You are not ready for dialogue because you think you are the only ones who are right. You think that anyone who asks you why, is an enemy who must be eliminated, and that is not right. No one has the monopoly of the truth."

They said those they kill are what they called "black legs" and "traitors" who are in league with the enemy.

"How different are you from them," I asked, "if you kill your own people simply because they disagree with your tactics, or because you suspect them of complicity with the army? How different do you think you are from the army you accuse of killing your people and destroying your homes when you, in turn, are doing exactly the same thing to the very people who are also victims of army exactions? Aren't you and the army doing exactly the same thing, victimising your own poor people?"

There was total silence in the room. Where at first,

they looked and behaved intimidatingly arrogant, they now sat with eyes downcast. "When you talk to someone, my dear children, and he says no, ask yourself why he is saying no, and listen to him. Don't just get up and put a bullet in his head as an enemy, or a traitor, or a blackleg, which is what is happening in groups like yours throughout the country." The silence intensified.

"The second point I disagree with you," I broke the silence, "is your position not to allow our children to go back to school. What you are now doing is fighting against your younger brothers and sisters and depriving them of a fundamental right to education, the right to build their future. What type of country are you fighting to build?" I asked. "If you don't let our children, your younger brothers and sisters, go to school, who will run the country you tell me you're fighting to build? Where have you ever seen a country in the modern world that is run by illiterates? Where? Tell me!"

After a moment of silence during which gazes were exchanged, one of them then stepped in to ask, "Do you prefer children to go to school and be killed, as it happened in Kumba recently, or to stay back home and be safe?"

"Frankly, I prefer to see children in school than at home," I told them, "even at the risk that they would be killed. You can quote me, I stand by my word. Yes, allow them to go to school. By the way, who is killing our children who are going to school? Is it not you?"

They were taken aback and frantically denied that

they kill school children. "No, no, it isn't us, it is "La Republique" that is killing school children, not us!"

"Leave our children alone; let them go back to school," I told them. "They are the ones to run your republic tomorrow, if you ever get one."

They sat in stunned silence, many of them with their eyes on their toes. Then one of them said, "We believe in a republic without schools."

"Are you serious?" I asked. "What part of the world are you living in, my friend? You want a country without education? Seriously?"

When I got no answer, I then raised the third point of my disagreement with them and their sponsors.

"My third point is a message I am sending to those who are sponsoring you from abroad, from Europe or North America. Let me give you one example of what I mean. One of your supporters happens to be a relative of mine. He once called me to boast of how he and his friends collect money each month for those of you fighting in the forests and bushes. I told him he had no idea how much harm he and his friends are doing to our people back home; how much suffering and hardship their actions are causing our people. I asked him to come back home and go to the forest with his wife and children and see for himself the sad reality of life in the forests. The reality of life you are living here in this bush. See where you live. I don't believe any of you is happy to live out here even if you don't admit it."

One of them then said, "We are forced to live out

here because of the actions of "La Republique!"

"That is exactly the same accusation I hear from my relative," I told him. "He lives thousands of miles from here; his children are attending school, he and his wife are working and making a decent living, but they collect money for you so you can use to buy arms with which you prevent your own children from going to school. His own children are attending school where he is. When I told him what I had in my mind, he has not talked to me since. Those of them out of the country, who are sending money to you, or who claim they are sending money to fund this war, have no idea of the reality on the ground."

They all looked visibly uneasy as they listened to me. I relished the opportunity I had to tell them exactly where I thought they are wrong.

"But before you start thinking that I am supporting the Cameroon government, against which you are fighting," I continued, "know that the same government has never trusted my actions. It has always suspected me of supporting those of you who are in the bushes. But, I don't care what anyone may think of me, whether the government or those of you, fighting in the bushes. My stand is clear: whether the violence against our people is from the government side, or from your side, it is wrong and unacceptable! I will say so to anyone who cares to listen, whether a government minister or a fighter in the bush. Our people are simply fed up with this war! They need and deserve peace, not death, not violence, not the destruction of their homes and property. Whenever I have an opportunity to talk to anyone in government, or to you people and your sponsors abroad, I am always very clear as to where I stand. Whether the government suspects me of siding with you is of no consequence to me; and whether you think I am supporting the government, is no concern of mine either. I am a pastor and I stand for peace in this land, which belongs to us all."

When I finished talking, there was complete silence in the room and I had a feeling that they had nothing more to say. I could sense that they were rather baffled by my frank talk to them. Then one of them said they had heard I was a supporter of a "one and indivisible Cameroon". I told them I did not know what the government slogan of "one and indivisible" meant but that I am a fervent supporter of a federation for Cameroon, not a separated Cameroon. Once more, silence descended on my audience and it was clear to me that there was some soul searching going on among them.

They then changed their style by asking me, to affirm for public consumption, that I had not been tortured, which was true. I did not, however, fail to remind them that keeping a 90-year-old man under such dreadful conditions for the night, and without any food, or his medicine, was a form of torture. They then asked that I confirm that no ransom had been paid for my release, which was true.

They again said that they expected me, once released, to serve as their 'spokesman' to the Cameroon government, and to the world at large. They expected me to refute the government's portrayal of them as terrorists instead of what they claimed to be, that is, freedom fighters, fighting for their homeland. I told them that I could not be a bearer of such a message because I did not have any facts to prove, or confirm, what they were telling me.

I again asked where the Fon was, telling them that I had come with him and I intended to go up to his palace with him. They reiterated what they had said earlier, namely, that they had handed him over to the "Nso Warriors", who had taken him home with them. They assured me, and it turned out to be false, that they were sure we would meet him already in his palace in Kumbo.

As I spoke to those fellows that morning, I looked at each of them carefully to see what type of people I was dealing with. I felt the oldest was in his forties and the youngest in his thirties. They looked and sounded much more mature, physically and even intellectually, than some of those I have met in Nsoland. The Bishop of Kumbo and I once met some of them in Wainama, who were just kids of school age playing with guns. The Bishop gave them a few francs and they went away singing and dancing. It was sad to see kids, who should have been in school, holding guns, looking so wretched, and it was clear to me that they had no idea why they were even out there in the bushes. I had a similar feeling of pity for those young people in the bush in Ndop who also looked and sounded as confused as those in Nso. I left wishing this war would end soon so they could leave the bushes and go back to school.

CHAPTER 10

Call the Governor

When the interview was over, our captors then asked me to call the Governor to tell him not to try to intervene to free me. They said they knew the army was not far from where we were but that they meant me no harm. However, it would be a fatal mistake if the army were to attack in an attempt to rescue me as there would likely be bloodshed, which they did not want to see happen. They said they would soon release me and my driver unharmed, but they could not guarantee what could happen if the army tried to intervene. Then one of them dialled the Governor's phone number and gave me the phone, and I passed him their message. He said he had understood, and that the army would not intervene.

When I saw that they doubted the Governor's sincerity, I asked why they did not choose a different route from the one they had taken the previous day to bring us where we were. They thought that was a good idea and so they made us sit on a bike and I again suffered the indignity and inconvenience of being transported through the rough farmland roads of the Ndop plain before being abandoned near the village of Chikong in Babessi, several miles away from where we had spent the night. As soon as the bikers dropped us off, they turned around and fled at full speed back into the bush.

FIGURE 10.1. Photo snapped by my captors

My Gratitude to the Woman with a Chair

I sat on the grass while my driver was trying to call people he knew to tell them we had been freed but that we were not sure where we were. It was then that something happened for which I remain eternally grateful. As I sat on the grass, a woman carrying a baby in her arms, and who had seen them drop us off, handed her baby to another woman and hurried to bring me a chair. She then asked us if we would like to have *fufu corn* and *njama-njama* for breakfast. We thanked her for her generosity but declined her offer of breakfast. I do not think she realised how deeply I appreciated her gesture. It was an extremely touching act of generosity on the part of a poor woman, who gave all that she had to a tired old man. Even though I do not believe she recognised me, she must have suspected, from my soutane, that I was a priest, accompanied by an altar boy, my driver, who had been captured and then released near her home.

I should add that, a few weeks later, as we were going back to Douala from Kumbo, this time being escorted by the army, I insisted on being taken back to that village for me to thank that woman for what she did for us.

She offered me a chair, which was a great relief for me, and breakfast of *fufu corn* and *njama-njama*, which we graciously declined. When I first mentioned the village in question, no one seemed to know exactly where it was until my driver remembered that someone had talked of a farm, belonging to former Prime Minister Philemon Yang, not far from there. It was then that someone knew where it was and its name, Chikong. It is about five kilometres from the main road, and I was glad to meet the generous woman we were looking for, and to thank her for her kindness to us.

FIGURE 10.2. A crowd comes out to celebrate my release from captivity

CHAPTER 11

Free at Last

That morning of our release, as we were still talking with the generous woman who had offered me a chair, another woman, who was passing by, stopped and greeted us in Lamnso. She said there was a huge crowd of several hundreds of people around a car they said belonged to the Cardinal several miles away from where we were. She was still describing what she had seen when some cars suddenly arrived and I saw some young men descend from them dressed in soutanes. They introduced themselves as priests of the Diocese of Kumbo and said they had been searching for us. They helped me get into one of the cars and when we arrived near my car, I saw crowds of people: priests, religious, and laity alike, as well as the traditional authorities of the locality, led by the Fon of Baba himself. He greeted me very warmly and said he and his people were delighted we had been released unharmed. He vowed that if the Fon of Nso was still within his jurisdiction, he was going to make sure that he was released, unharmed as well.

It was a heart-warming moment for me and I greatly appreciated his kind words to us on behalf of his people of Baba. Having spent the night in pitch darkness in a rundown farmhouse, at the mercy of mosquitoes, feeling lonely and abandoned and wondering if we would ever see the light of day again, there we were, being welcomed by such a multitude of people expressing their joy in song and prayer. That was quite a scene! I began to recognize a few faces around. I saw the Divisional Officer of Kumbo, the young man, who, the day before, had brought us the Governor's offer of a military escort, which we had turned down.

Later, when we arrived in Kumbo, I was eager to meet the Fon, who should already have been in his palace. My disappointment was understandably great when I realised that our captors had lied to me about his being already released! Not knowing exactly where he was, or what had happened to him, was a source of great pain and anxiety for me. I decided to stay in Kumbo until he was released. It was two days later that I heard that he had finally been let go and had, of his own free will, decided to go back to Bamenda, for medical treatment, instead of coming up to his palace. I thanked God Almighty for sparing his life.

The next day, I left for Bamenda where I met him and he said he, his wife and *nchelav* had been worried that something bad might have happened to us. I told him we, too, had been worried about them, and that all was well that ended well. The Governor came to meet us at the hotel where the Fon was. He expressed his relief at seeing us but had a good laugh, all the same, because we had turned down his offer of a military escort up to Nso. Our discussion was light-hearted, and I left feeling happy that I had met the Fon again under more pleasant circumstances.

CHAPTER 12

Conclusion

At the beginning of this conflict, the government thought that I was against it and in support of the "Amba boys"; for their part, the "Amba boys" thought I was with the government. This is a clear indication, if any were needed, of the neutrality of my position. For a long time, I wondered how the situation would end. But then I met an elderly woman just before the Major National Dialogue, who showed me the way. She is a retired teacher, who refused to leave her village of Mbiame in Nsoland even at the height of the killings and massive destruction of homes and other property. I was preparing to attend the Major National Dialogue and I asked her what she thought we could do for peace to return, and for our children to go back to school. She gave a very short answer: "Let the army go back to the barracks with their guns, and let these boys drop their own guns, which they are holding illegally. Then there will be peace and schools will resume." When I asked who she thought could send the army back to the barracks, her response was loud and clear: "No one else but the President of the Republic, Mr. Paul Biya." In that short statement, she merely echoed what I have always believed to be the solution to this seemingly interminable conflict.

As this war drags on, with seemingly no end in sight, I continue to reflect on what should happen if the army were to go back to the barracks and the "Amba boys" refuse to surrender their arms. The more I think of it, the more I am convinced that if the army were to withdraw to the barracks and the "Amba boys" refuse to disarm, the army, which is known for imposing order and discipline, should come out of the barracks and take over power in the country for a short period of time. After imposing order and discipline, it should then organise elections, return power to the civilians and withdraw to their barracks, where they rightfully belong.

Lest I be misunderstood, I have personally never been in favour of military rule anywhere. However, where human lives and property are being wasted, as it is the case in our country, an army take-over could be the lesser of two evils. This conflict is dragging on for too long and causing untold damage in human lives and property.

The Human Side of our Captors

I will not end without saying something about what I saw as the human side of our captors. The situation could have ended tragically for us since they were armed and nervous, knowing well that the army was around, and could intervene at any time. I saw how worried they were, afraid that something bad could happen to us. They feared possible bloodshed if the army were to intervene, something they did not want to see happen to us. I felt that they were not so much worried about themselves as they were about me, an old man and a priest, whom they were beginning to find rather cumbersome in their hands.

When I talk of the 'human side' of these children in the bushes, I remember one I met in Kikai, who told me that they were no longer sure of what they were fighting for. There is no longer any clear, defined purpose for their struggle. Some of those who held us captive said just as much, they have lost track of the purpose for which they are fighting. A few of them even gave my driver their phone numbers and, weeks later, without waiting for him to call them, they called him to ask how I was doing and asked him to greet me. They then told him that they had nothing to eat and wondered if he could be of any assistance to them.

In all truthfulness, I too wonder, with these boys, what this struggle is for now. It is high time the guns fell silent so we can bury our loved ones and embark on the reconstruction of our land. There can be no victor in this war. Should it persist, we will all emerge as losers. Let peace reign in our land!

My Gratitude for your Sympathy

I will not like to end this reflection without thanking all of you, who prayed for our release. To you, who walked for miles from Nso all the way to where my car was found, waiting in prayer for our release, I say thank you! To you, who, from around the world, stood up for us, I say thank you! Even without knowing who I was, great numbers of people in our country, and worldwide, expressed their sympathy, prayed for our release, and sent me countless messages of good will. Now I have an idea of what will happen when the Lord finally calls me home. I thank you all and I have you in my prayers. Remember to pray for me as well.

About the Author

Christian Cardinal Wiyghan Tumi was born on 15 October 1930 in Kikaikelaki, a small village in Nsoland in the Northwest Region of English-speaking Cameroon. He did his seminary studies in Nigeria, then went on to earn a licentiate in theology in Lyon, France, and a doctorate in philosophy at the University of Fribourg, Switzerland. Ordained a priest on 17 April 1966, he served in many capacities in the Diocese of Buea before being appointed the first Rector of the sole Major Seminary in Bambui in the English-speaking part of Cameroon.

Pope John Paul II appointed him the first bishop of the Diocese of Yagoua in 1979. In 1984, he was appointed the Archbishop of Garoua and was created a Cardinal-Priest in 1988. He was named the Archbishop of Douala on 31 August 1991 where he served until his retirement. He recently celebrated his 90th birthday anniversary a few months before being abducted, and held overnight, by secessionist forces in the restive English-speaking Northwest Region of Cameroon. That abduction is the subject of this publication.

About the Publisher

Spears Books is an independent publisher dedicated to providing innovative publication strategies with emphasis on African/Africana stories and perspectives. As a platform for alternative voices, we prioritize the accessibility and affordability of our titles in order to ensure that relevant and often marginal voices are represented at the global marketplace of ideas. Our titles – poetry, fiction, narrative nonfiction, memoirs, reference, travel writing, African languages, and young people's literature – aim to bring African worldviews closer to diverse readers. Our titles are distributed in paperback and electronic formats globally by African Books Collective.

Connect with Us

Visit our Website

Go to www.spearsmedia.com to learn about exclusive previews and read excerpts of new books, find detailed information on our titles, authors, subject area books, and special discounts.

Subscribe to our Free Newsletter

Be amongst the first to hear about our newest publications, special discount offers, news about bestsellers, author interviews, coupons and more! Subscribe to our newsletter by visiting www.spearsmedia.com

Quantity Discounts

Spears books are available at quantity discounts for orders of ten or more copies. Contact Spears Books at orders@spearsmedia.com.

Host a Reading Group

Learn more about how to host a reading group on our website at www.spearsmedia.com

Printed in the United States
by Baker & Taylor Publisher Services

Printed in the United States
by Baker & Taylor Publisher Services